WELCOME TO ALI THE ALLIGATORS' SWAMP

Coloring Books Kids

EDUCANDO KIDS

Let's color
these alligator
coloring pages!

This is a Bleed Through Page If You Are Using a Coloring Marker or Pen!
Find Other Great Titles By searching for Educando Kids on Your Favorite Book Retailer
Amazon.Com | Barnes & Noble (BN.Com) | Books A Million (BAM.Com)

EDUCANDO
KIDS

Printed in the USA
CPSIA information can be obtained
at www.ICGtesting.com
LVHW051115181023
761372LV00035B/435